D0975515

‹TANZANIA›

MAJOR WORLD NATIONS

TANZANIA

Withdrawn

Patricia E. McCulla

CHELS   S

Chelsea House Publishers

Contributing Author: Tom Purdom

Copyright © 1999 by Chelsea House Publishers,
a subsidiary of Haights Cross Communications.
All rights reserved.
Printed and bound in Malaysia.

3 5 7 9 8 6 4

Library of Congress Cataloging-in-Publication Data

McCulla, Patricia E.
Tanzania.
Includes index.

Summary: Discusses the history, geography, industry, culture, and people
of the large East African country.

1. Tanzania—Juvenile literature. [1. Tanzania]
I. Title
DT438.M37   1988   967.8   87-18241
ISBN 0-7910-4768-7

◄CONTENTS►

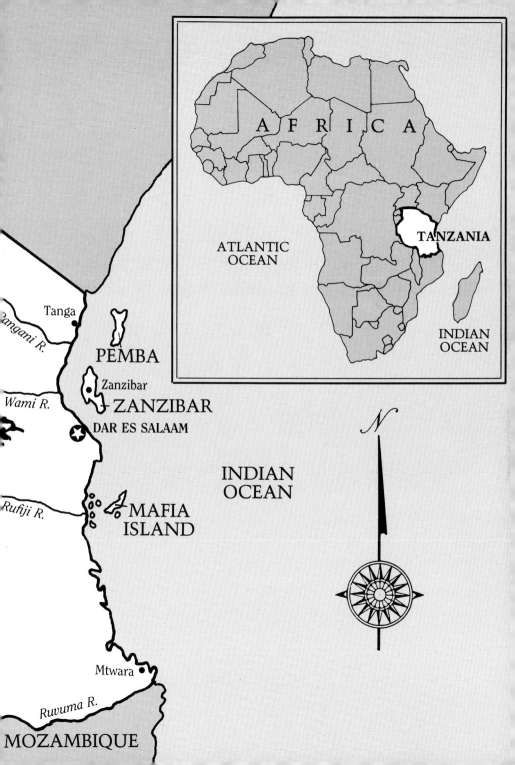

◄ FACTS AT A GLANCE ►

Land and People

Area	365,000 square miles (945,000 square kilometers)
Highest Point	Mount Kilimanjaro, 19,340 feet (5,895 meters)
Major Islands	Zanzibar, Pemba
Major Lakes	Victoria, Tanganyika, Rukwa, Nyasa, Natron, Manyara, Eyasi
Major Rivers	Rufiji, Ruvu, Great Ruaha, Wami, Pangani, Ruvuma, Malagarasi, Kilombero, Gombe
Capital	Dar es Salaam
Major Cities	Mwanza, Dodoma, Tanga, Zanzibar, Arusha
Population	29,000,000
Population Distribution	Rural, 77 percent; urban, 23 percent
National Language	Swahili; English is the primary language of commerce, administration, and higher education; Kinguiji (a form of Swahili) and Arabic are spoken on Zanzibar
Literacy Rate	68 percent
Ethnic Groups	African (99 percent), Asian, European, Arab
Religion	Christian, approximately 44 percent; Muslim, 37 percent (99 percent on Zanzibar); traditional religions, 19 percent
Life Expectancy	42 years

Economy

Agriculture — Accounts for 58 percent of the gross domestic product, 85 percent of export earnings, and 90 percent of employment

Major Export Crops — Coffee, cotton, tobacco, tea, cashew nuts, sisal, cloves from Zanzibar

Industry — Accounts for 8 percent of gross domestic product

Major Industrial Products — Agricultural and brewing products (including sugar, beer, cigarettes, and sisal twine), textiles, cement, shoes

Currency — Tanzanian shilling

Per Capita Gross Domestic Product — Equal to US $800

Government

Form of Government — Republic

Head of State — President (Zanzibar has a separate president who heads the island's internal affairs)

Legislature — 274-member National Assembly: 232 members elected for five-year terms; 42 seats filled by presidential appointment or reserved by law for specific officials

Prime Minister — Appointed by the president

Cabinet — Appointed by the president from members of the National Assembly

◄HISTORY AT A GLANCE►

2 million B.C.	Australopithecines, upright-walking primates who were ancestors of modern man, occupy Tanzania.
before 300 B.C.	Mainland Tanzania is inhabited by Pygmy-like people related to the Khoisan of southern Africa. The Cush-ites, Bantu, and Nilotes migrate into the area in waves, bringing farming, ironworking, and herding skills. On the islands of Zanzibar and Pemba, Bantu descendants intermarry with Arab and Persian trad-ers. Their offspring are the Swahili people, who inhabit the mainland coast, and the Shirazi people of the islands.
12th century A.D.	Under the Shirazi, the coastal city of Kilwa becomes East Africa's most important trading center.
1500	Mainland society develops into a network of chief-doms led by royal families. Over the next three centu-ries, the chiefdoms become powerful political bodies. A caste system begins to develop.
16th century	Portuguese traders arrive on the coast of East Africa. They gain control of the coast and Zanzibar Island, and they set up trading posts.
1698	Omani Arabs take control of Portuguese trading centers at Mombasa, Kenya, and Zanzibar. The mainland's coastal cities become important centers of Arab trade and culture. The economy revolves around the slave trade.
19th century	Trade between mainland African tribes and the Arab and Swahili people of the coast increases. Three major trade routes are developed. Some mainland

Africans capture and sell slaves to the Arab and Swahili traders.

1884 Carl Peters of the German Colonization Society lays German claim to large areas of the mainland.

1885 German leader Otto von Bismarck declares the area held by Peters to be a German protectorate.

1891 Germany formally makes the mainland a colony. The sultan of Zanzibar asks Britain for help against the Germans. The British declare Zanzibar a British protectorate.

1905 to 1908 Mainland Africans rebel against German rule during the Maji Maji Rebellion.

1917 During World War I, British troops drive the Germans from the mainland.

1922 Under the terms of the League of Nations, Britain takes control of the mainland, now called Tanganyika.

1925 Sir Donald Cameron becomes governor of Tanganyika. He gives some local government tasks to Tanganyikans under a policy of indirect rule.

1926 The British introduce a Legislative Council on Zanzibar.

1929 African civil servants in Tanganyika form the African Association, a labor organization that eventually becomes a political power.

1940 The Tanganyika African Association (TAA) holds its first territorial conference.

1946 At the end of World War II, the United Nations makes Tanganyika a Trust Territory of Britain. Britain is told to make the colony ready for independence.

mid-1950s The independence movement gains strength on Zanzibar. Several parties and organizations are formed to promote independence.

1954   The TAA becomes the Tanganyika African National Union (TANU), an organization dedicated to independence from British rule. Julius Nyerere is elected TANU's president.

1957   General elections for the Legislative Council are held in Zanzibar; the pro-independence Zanzibar Nationalist party wins a majority of seats.

1958 and 1959   TANU wins large majorities in Tanganyika's general elections for the Legislative Council.

1960   The British ask Nyerere to become chief minister of Tanganyika and to form a new government after Nyerere's party wins the Legislative Council elections again.

1961   Tanganyika declares its independence. The country becomes a member of the Commonwealth of Nations (an association including Great Britain and many former British colonies). The government changes the country's name to Tanzania. On Zanzibar, the Zanzibar Nationalist party again wins a majority of seats in the Legislative Council.

1962   Julius Nyerere resigns as prime minister of Tanzania. Later in the year a constitutional change makes Tanzania a republic with a president as head of state.

1963   Zanzibar becomes independent. The new government is controlled by Arabs. On the mainland, Nyerere returns to public life and is elected president.

1964   A rebellion led by African residents of Zanzibar overthrows the Arab government in January. More than 5,000 Arabs are killed in fighting. In April, the revolutionary government of Zanzibar and Pemba forms a union with Tanzania under the name Tanzania.

1967   President Nyerere announces the Arusha Declaration, which outlines principles of socialism and economic self-reliance for Tanzania. On Zanzibar, living con-

Almost one-quarter of Tanzania's territory is occupied by wildlife preserves and game parks.

ditions and civil rights deteriorate under a strict dictatorship.

1972   Abeid Karume, Zanzibar's head of government, is assassinated.

1977   The main political parties of the mainland and Zanzibar merge to form the Chama Cha Mapinduzi (Revolutionary party).

1978   Uganda and Tanzania go to war over disputed borders.

1979   Tanzania invades Uganda and occupies the country until a new government is established.

1985   Ali Hassan Mwinyi is elected president of Tanzania after Nyerere says he is finally stepping down from office.

1986   The government begins a program to reduce state control of the economy.

1991   The Zanzibar Declaration begins reform of the political system.

1992   The government decides to adopt a multiparty democracy. Eleven political parties are registered.

1995   General elections are held.

These Tanzanians are working on a banana plantation near Dodoma. New plantings are shown in the foreground.

Tanzania
and the World

Tanzania is one of the most important countries in Africa. It was the first nation in East Africa to achieve independence, and it has played a pivotal role in African affairs. Its first president, Julius Nyerere, carried out an aggressive foreign policy and worked to build a sense of African unity, or pan-Africanism, among the new nations south of the Sahara. In Uganda, in 1977, the hated dictator Idi Amin was deposed from power because Nyerere sent Tanzanian troops into the country.

Tanzania's impressive natural beauty and its vast wildlife preserves also make this country special. The snow-capped peaks of Mount Kilimanjaro, Africa's tallest mountain, stand sentrylike over the northern plains. Nearby, lions and large herds of giraffe and zebra range across the Serengeti Plain and wildlife preserve.

A few miles offshore in the Indian Ocean lies Zanzibar, an island with a history of slavery and political intrigue. Zanzibar was a separate country until it united with the mainland of Tanzania in 1964. It still maintains a separate cultural and political identity within the Tanzanian federation.

Tanzania and Zanzibar are so different that only a remarkable man could have unified them. That man was Julius Nyerere. In many ways, the history of modern Tanzania is the story of Julius Nyerere's life, first as the leader of the independence movement and then as the architect of Tanzania's experiment with a socialist government and economy. Nyerere's charismatic leadership unified the Tanzanian people. He helped Tanzania avoid ethnic strife among the more than 130 different peoples that make up the country. Even after he left the presidency in 1985, Nyerere continued to influence the changes inaugurated by his successors.

After Tanzania became independent in 1962, Nyerere set up a one-party socialist system. He used the Swahili word *ujamaa* ("togetherness" or "familyhood") to describe the ideals his government was supposed to encourage. He believed he could create a uniquely African solution to the problems of ethnic division, limited political rights, and poverty.

Nyerere's policies led to some notable advances in social welfare, but the economy of Tanzania stagnated and the country became heavily dependent on foreign aid. In 1986, a new president, Ali Hassan Mwinyi, yielded to pressure from international organizations and transformed Tanzania's economic policies. Mwinyi adopted a market-oriented policy and began re-

Vocational training is one of the programs the Tanzanian government has sponsored to improve the economy.

ducing government control of the economic system. In 1993, the Tanzanian government also reformed the political system by allowing citizens to form political parties. In 1995, when Tanzania held its first multiparty election, four parties competed against the government party, the Revolutionary State party. Observers generally agreed that the voting was honest and fair. The government party won the election, but the other parties received over a third of the presidential vote and approximately 25 percent of the seats in Tanzania's parliament.

Today, Tanzania is still one of the poorest countries in Africa and the world, and it still depends on foreign aid and assistance to feed its people. It is still reducing government control of the economy, and it continues to struggle with the social problems that beset most African countries. Its economy has begun to grow, however, and the nation is beginning to attract foreign investment.

In just four decades, Tanzania has moved from colonialism to socialism to capitalism. It has replaced a colonial administration with a one-party political system and then transformed the one-party system into a full multiparty democracy. Yet, through all these transitions, the country has remained stable and peaceful. It has avoided the nightmarish dictatorships and the bloody ethnic violence that have troubled young countries all over the world. Though the nation has not yet achieved all the goals of its founders, it has become a dynamic presence on the African continent.

Workers harvest cotton, one of Tanzania's major export crops, near Dodoma.

The Land

The United Republic of Tanzania consists of a large mainland and several small islands. The mainland is bordered by the Indian Ocean to the east, by Kenya, Uganda, Rwanda, and Burundi to the north, by Mozambique, Malawi, and Zambia to the south, and by Congo to the west. The mainland has a total area of 365,000 square miles (945,000 square kilometers). About 23,000 square miles (59,000 sq km) of this is lakes and rivers. The largest and most important of the islands is Zanzibar. It is located 22 miles (35 km) from the mainland and covers about 640 square miles (1,660 sq km). Pemba, the second-largest island, lies 25 miles (40 km) northeast of Zanzibar, and covers about 380 square miles (985 sq km).

Tanzania's varied landscape includes mountains, valleys, plateaus, plains, rivers, and lakes. The central region of the mainland is a plateau capped by mountains in the north. The plateau is covered with scrub vegetation and areas of "sunk lands," where acacia (a woody plant with white or yellow flowers that is also called gum arabic) and tall grasses grow. The northern stretches of the plateau contain open woodland and evergreen forest.

Between the central plateau and the Indian Ocean is the east central region. It contains the nation's capital, Dar es Salaam. The coast has light, sandy soil; inland, large stretches are covered by dense thickets in which wild pigs, baboons, and monkeys live. The island of Mafia, just offshore, is considered part of this region.

North of the central plateau is a mountainous area with some of Africa's most important land features: Mount Kilimanjaro, the highest mountain in Africa at 19,340 feet (5,895 meters); the Olduvai Gorge, a huge rift or valley where archaeologists have unearthed remains of man's earliest ancestors; and part of the Serengeti Plain, one of Africa's most famous wildlife areas. The north central region also includes Lake Natron, Mount Meru, part of the Pangani River, and the East African Rift Valley, a series of depressions and crevices that cuts through much of East Africa.

The northeast region, surrounding the coastal town of Tanga, consists of a gently rising coastal plain. Much of the plain is limestone, a type of rock formed from organic materials such as coral or shells.

Lake Victoria, Africa's largest lake, juts into northwestern Tanzania. Much of the country's farmland is located in this region, because many of the nation's rivers drain into Lake Victoria, irrigating the land and making it suitable for farming.

The southern coast consists of either sandy or coral shoreline dotted with mangrove forests or low-lying areas covered with coconut palms, casuarinas, and scrub brush. The southwest is a region of woodlands, baobab trees, and thickets.

In the west, between Lake Tanganyika and the central plateau, are three geographical areas. The northern shore of the lake is a low-lying area drained by the Malagarasi River, which flows into the lake. The southern shore is covered by woodland. Between these two areas is the western highland region. It consists of a continuation of the central plateau, broken by the rugged, hilly Buha, Mpanda, and Ufipa highlands. Tsetse flies infest a large part of the western region. Because tsetse flies carry the tropical disease called sleeping sickness, which causes drowsiness and drastic weight loss, most of this area has been left uncultivated. The tsetse fly and inadequate rainfall are two of the primary reasons Tanzanians have cultivated only 5 percent of their land area.

The Mwanza–Musoma road leads to Mwanza, a city on the shore of Lake Victoria, the largest lake in Tanzania.

Tanzania's chief mountains are the Usambara and Kilimanjaro ranges in the northeast, the Mahali Mountains on the shore of Lake Tanganyika, the Poroto, Kipengere, and Livingstone ranges just north of Lake Nyasa, and the Nguru, Rubeho, and Uluguru ranges between the central plateau and the eastern lowlands. Mount Meru, southwest of Kilimanjaro, is the country's second-highest peak; it is 14,973 feet (4,565 meters) high.

Other important geographical features of the Tanzanian mainland include: the Masai Steppe, a broad, flat grassland in the northeast that is the home of the Masai people; the Bahi Swamp, a huge marshland on the eastern edge of the central plateau; and Speke Gulf, on the southeastern edge of Lake Victoria. Speke Gulf is named for John Hanning Speke, a British explorer who first identified Lake Victoria as the source of the White Nile River. After a difficult and hazardous crossing from the Indian Ocean coast, he reached the shores of Lake Victoria near the present-day city of Mwanza in 1858. His report of the vast lake lying hidden in the heart of Africa inspired many explorers to follow him.

The Islands

The coral-rock island of Zanzibar lies about 22 miles (35 kilometers) off the coast. It is mainly flat except for an irregular ridge that runs north to south. The soils to the east of the ridge are shallow and sandy; to the west, they are deeper and more fertile. The eastern area, called *wandaa* country, is noted for its grasslands, scrub vegetation, mangrove swamps, and coral rocks.

Zanzibar's west coast is sheltered by a coral reef and protected by the central ridge from the easterly winds and waves of the Indian Ocean; this makes the west coast a safe place to anchor boats throughout the year. The east coast faces the full force of the Indian Ocean and is not a safe anchorage.

Pemba, Tanzania's second-largest island, is located 25 miles (40 km) to the northeast of Zanzibar. Its valleys and uneven hillside terraces con-

Near Mwanza, workers take thousands of tiny Haplochromis fish from Lake Victoria. After drying in the sun, the fish can be stored or exported.

trast with Zanzibar's flat landscape. Pemba's soils are more fertile than Zanzibar's, because Pemba receives a heavier rainfall, which releases the natural nutrients found in the soil.

Lakes and Rivers

Tanzania is a land of lakes. Half of Lake Victoria, the largest body of water on the African continent, lies inside the northern border. Another of Africa's large lakes, Lake Tanganyika, lies along the border between Tanzania and Congo. Smaller lakes include Natron, Manyara, Eyasi, and Rukwa. Tanzania also claims part of Lake Nyasa (also called Lake Malawi), a huge lake that forms a large part of the neighboring country of Malawi, but Malawi and most other nations do not recognize this claim.

Only a few large rivers flow through Tanzania. The largest is the Rufiji River, which flows across southern Tanzania into the Indian Ocean. The

Rufiji's water flow is large enough to irrigate much of the nation and provide hydroelectric power, if it is harnessed through dams and canals. Three other large rivers also drain into the Indian Ocean: the Wami, which flows from the Nguru Mountains; the Pangani, which flows from the Kilimanjaro and Usambara mountains; and the Ruvuma, which forms Tanzania's southern border. A dam across the Pangani provides electricity for the towns of Arusha, Moshi, Tanga, Morogoro, and Dar es Salaam. Another large river is the Great Ruaha, which meets the Rufiji in eastern Tanzania. Most of Tanzania's other rivers, including the Gombe and the Kilombero, drain into Lakes Tanganyika, Victoria, or Nyasa.

Climate

The temperature on the Tanzanian mainland varies with the altitude. It ranges from tropical at sea level to temperate in the highlands and mountains. The climate can be divided into four categories: the hot and humid coastal plains; the hot and dry central plateau; the high, moist lake region; and the temperate highlands. Temperatures vary greatly, from an annual average of 68° Fahrenheit (20° Centigrade) in the highlands to an average of 90° F (32° C) on the coast.

Most of the country has one rainy season, which lasts from December to May. Some areas have two rainy seasons: from October to November and from April to May. Rainfall varies by region. The central plateau, for example, receives an uncertain amount of rainfall that averages about 25 inches (635 millimeters) a year, while the shores of Lakes Tanganyika and Victoria receive about 40 inches (1,016 mm) a year. Some areas in the southern highlands receive as much as 100 inches (2,540 mm) annually.

The mainland's weather is governed by monsoons, heavy winds that blow across the country twice a year. The northeast monsoon blows from December to March, bringing the hottest temperatures of the year. The southwest monsoon, from June through September, brings cool weather.

Like the mainland, Zanzibar and Pemba are affected by the northeast and southwest monsoons. But they get much more rain than the mainland. The *masika*, or "greater rains," occur from mid-March until the end of May, and the *mvuli*, or "lesser rains," occur from October to December. Zanzibar averages between 60 and 70 inches (1,524 to 1,778 millimeters) of rainfall per year, whereas Pemba receives more than 70 inches (1,778 mm).

The temperatures of Zanzibar and Pemba are similar to temperatures on the coastal mainland. They range from about 75° F (24° C) to 85° F (29° C). Steady winds that blow from the Indian Ocean help make the heat bearable.

Many important discoveries have been made by paleoanthropologists (scientists who study early man) on the edge of the great Serengeti Plain.

Early History

Mainland Tanzania and the island of Zanzibar have been united only for the past few decades. Before then they were separate countries, each with its own history, culture, and language. The mixture of Zanzibar's Arab heritage and the mainland's African culture has given modern Tanzania a flavor unique in eastern Africa. The history of Tanzania is one of two cultures moving toward unity—and toward independence from outside powers.

Tanzania's earliest history begins on the mainland. Scientists believe that Tanzania may have been one of the first homes of modern man's remote ancestors. Since the late 1950s, paleoanthropologists (scientists who study fossils and other traces of early humans) have made several important discoveries in Tanzania that shed light on the beginnings of human history.

The first of these discoveries took place in northern Tanzania on the edge of the great Serengeti Plain. There a great rift in the earth called the Olduvai Gorge marks the course of an ancient river. The area is rich in the fossils of tiny horses, giant giraffes, and other extinct creatures that lived along the river banks millions of years ago. In 1959, paleoanthropologists Louis and Mary Leakey discovered the fossil jawbone of a new species that belonged to the group of hominids (small, upright-walking manlike creatures) known as *Australopithecus*. The Leakeys later found other fossils that showed this early hominid had a brain similar to those of the great apes. But its most distinguishing feature was its huge, powerful jaws. The new species, which lived in Olduvai Gorge between one million and two million years ago, was named *Zinjanthropus*, but quickly became known as Nutcracker Man because of its strong jaws.

In 1964, the Leakeys found fossils of another species of hominid at Olduvai Gorge. The fossils showed that the new hominid had a larger brain than Nutcracker Man, but the most exciting part of the find was the stone tools found with the fossils. The tools were made for stabbing, cutting, and scraping. This new species was evidently the world's first toolmaker. The Leakeys named the hominid *Homo habilis*, or Handy Man, in honor of its use of tools. Many paleoanthropologists today believe that *Homo habilis* is modern man's direct ancestor. It, too, is more than a million years old.

Twenty miles (32 kilometers) south of Olduvai Gorge is an area called Laetoli (its name is the Masai word for the red lily that grows in the region). In 1976, a team of scientists working here with Mary Leakey made an extraordinary discovery—they found the preserved footprints of perhaps the oldest known hominids. These footprints tell fragments of an ancient story.

About 3.7 million years ago, a pair of hominids walked upright along a lakeshore. The larger one was probably male; the smaller one, probably female, walked behind the male and may have been carrying something— perhaps an infant. The clay soil was wet, and they left clear footprints in the mud. Soon after they passed, a nearby volcano (today called Sadiman) spewed forth clouds of hot ash that covered and preserved the footprints. Because nothing disturbed them, they turned to stone. They are the oldest such traces yet found of man's distant ancestors.

Over millions of years, these ancient hominids evolved into modern man *(Homo sapiens)* in Tanzania and elsewhere. Scientists now believe that modern man first spread throughout mainland Tanzania about

35,000 years ago. These early inhabitants were a short, slender people with light brown skin and curly hair. Physically they resembled the modern-day Pygmies who live in the rain forests of Zaire and the Khoikhoi and San peoples (sometimes called Khoisan or Bushmen) who live in the Kalahari region of southern Africa. These prehistoric Tanzanians were nomads who built no permanent settlements. Family bands migrated in search of game and survived by hunting and gathering wild plants. They may have spoken a language similar to the Khoisan language, in which many words have a "click" sound.

These people were slowly absorbed by a group of newcomers from the north who spoke a language similar to the Cushitic language of Ethiopia. The Cushitic people introduced cattle herding and farming. Then, around 500 B.C., Bantu-speaking people migrated from the rain forests of the west to the region near Lake Victoria. The Bantu-speaking groups were farmers who knew how to forge iron into weapons and tools. The Bantu slowly pushed south and east from Lake Victoria and colonized main-land Tanzania over the next several centuries.

During the Bantu migration, another ethnic group entered Tanzania. The new group was called the Nilotes, because they came from the south-ern Sudan, along the Nile River. The Nilotes, whose descendants today include the Masai people, were warriors and cattle-herding nomads. Like the Cushitic peoples, the Nilotes were outnumbered by the Bantu. For the most part, the Nilote peoples pursued their nomadic way of life in isolated regions of northern Tanzania, remote from the growing centers of Bantu influence. Over the years, however, some intermingling of these peoples and cultures did take place.

During this period of colonization, several important political and social changes occurred. The Bantu created a political system of small chiefdoms, or tribal states, dominated by royal families who were orga-nized into clans. The royal families were believed to be appointed by the gods. Between 1500 and 1800 A.D., these chiefdoms grew larger and more powerful.

The most important social change was the introduction of the caste system, in which the people who belonged to different tribal groups within Bantu society were divided into "higher" and "lower" social classes. The caste system gave rise to the clientship system, in which an individual from a lower social class offered his services to a member of a higher social class in return for certain privileges, such as military protection.

The Bantu chiefdoms constantly fought among one another over territory. In the 19th century, the royal families began enlisting warriors to help them support their claims. The warriors became a powerful force, forming their own social class. In time, the warrior class had greater political power than the royal families.

A Masai herdsman gathers firewood. The Masai are descended from the Nilote peoples who settled in Tanzania around 500 B.C.

The formation and growth of the chiefdoms marked an important development in mainland history. As the chiefdoms grew in size and power, they came into contact with traders from the islands of Zanzibar and Pemba. This contact between the mainland people and the Zanzibar traders set the stage for the invasion of the mainland by Arabs and Europeans.

The Rise of Zanzibar

The original inhabitants of Zanzibar and Pemba were probably Bantus who migrated from the mainland. Their descendants, the Tumbatu and Hadimu tribes on Zanzibar and the wa-Pemba on Pemba, intermarried with Persian traders from what is now known as Iran and with Arabs from other parts of the Middle East. The children of these intermarriages were known as the Shirazi.

In the 12th century, the Shirazi became the rulers of Kilwa, a city on the mainland. The Shirazi made Kilwa the greatest trading center on the East African coast. By the middle of the 13th century, Kilwa controlled the gold trade with Mozambique. The Shirazi traders exchanged the gold for cloth, metal wares, spices, and other goods from Arabia and India. Soon, however, Kilwa began to lose its control of the coastal trade.

By the end of the 15th century, Arab traders in Mombasa, Kenya, had made that city the largest trading center of the East African coast. Kilwa's Shirazi traders were cut out of this lucrative trade circuit, so they focused their energies on trade between Kilwa and Zanzibar. This new trade route became important when the Portuguese came to the East African coast in the 16th century.

With their superior weaponry and ships, the Portuguese seized control of the East African trading centers from the Arabs. They then prevented Arab merchants from trading at important ports, such as Sofala in Mozambique. With the loss of the seaborne trade, the Arab merchants turned to the tribes on the mainland and began trading foodstuffs for ivory, beeswax (for candles), rhinoceros horn, and animal skins. Swahili, a language mixing Arabic and African words, became the common trading language in the area. The descendants of Arab traders who intermarried with Africans living on the coast were called Swahilis.

In 1698, Arabs from Oman pushed the Portuguese out of the trading areas in Kenya and Tanzania and made Zanzibar the center of their trading activity. The island became the base for trade along the entire mainland coast. Coastal towns revived and new settlements arose because of the lively commerce.

When an Arab named Sayyid Said became sultan (ruler) of Zanzibar, the coastal towns enjoyed increased commercial activity. He attracted Asian merchants, especially Indians, to the island. The Asians soon played a pivotal role in trade, because they made massive loans to Arab merchants. The Arabs needed the money to finance the trade caravans they sent into the interior of the mainland. At first the Arabs traded for iron, ivory, and salt, but within a few years they found their most profitable trade item: slaves. Thousands of black Africans from the interior were taken to slave markets in Zanzibar and elsewhere.

The Arab traders established three major inland trade routes: from the coastal city of Bagamoyo to Ujiji, a major trading center located on the shore of Lake Tanganyika; from Tanga toward Mt. Kilimanjaro; and into the Lake Malawi region from Kilwa. These routes allowed the coastal Arab and Swahili merchants—as well as the Bantu chieftains who helped them in slave raids—to establish great political power over the interior.

Arab domination of the interior was abruptly interrupted in the late 19th century, when Carl Peters, a representative of the German Colonization Society, decided that Germany should join the other European countries that were scrambling to claim parts of Africa. Peters set his sights on mainland Tanzania. He arrived in Dar es Salaam in 1884 and secretly traveled inland. Within three weeks, 12 illiterate chiefs had signed their lands over to Peters.

The Age of Imperialism

Peters laid German claim to Tanzania at a time when European interest in Africa was at a fever pitch. An economic depression, a need for new markets for manufactured goods, and the prestige of holding colonial territory had driven Great Britain, France, Belgium, Italy, Portugal, and Germany to compete with one another to control Africa. The European nations carved Africa up like an enormous pie and quarreled over the pieces.

The British had good relations with the sultan of Zanzibar. They watched cautiously as Peters claimed coastal Tanzania for Germany. Germany's chancellor, Otto von Bismarck, disliked Peters, but he realized that Peters's treaties gave Germany a powerful foothold in Africa; he also realized that other nations could easily seize that foothold.

In 1884, Bismarck convened a conference of European nations in Berlin to lay the ground rules for European colonization in Africa. The Berlin Conference participants reached agreement on how the Europeans would rule Africa: a European nation could claim an African territory only by setting up a colony in the territory.

The 19th-century German conquerors of Tanzania often gave local authority to native rulers like this former sultan.

When the conference ended in 1885, Bismarck quickly adopted the conference rules and immediately declared the region governed by the German East Africa Company, the successor to Peters's group, to be a German protectorate (this meant that the German government would protect the territory by military force, if necessary). With this protection the German East Africa Company began to extend the borders of its new territory. Germany signed a treaty with Great Britain that gave Britain control of Zanzibar in return for total German control of the mainland. Zanzibari Arabs living in the coastal settlements were not so easily won over, and fighting broke out between the Arabs and the Germans.

The German East African Company could not defeat the Arabs, and in 1889, Bismarck sent German troops to the territory. Bitter fighting continued for almost a year until all the Arab coastal towns—including Kilwa—were under German control. But the German troops did not return home once the fighting ended; instead, they began to march toward the interior along the caravan routes. On January 1, 1891, the German government officially took control of the interior as well as the coast and the German colonization of Tanzania began in earnest.

It took the Germans eight years to conquer the peoples of Tanzania. Once the caravan routes were secured, German troops and *askaris* (black African troops who fought for the Germans) fought and negotiated their way to the north, south, and west. The many peoples who lived in Tanzania reacted differently to the German forces. Some quietly accepted German rule without fighting; others negotiated with the Germans to allow local tribal government; and some refused to submit and fought off the approaching German troops. Tanzanian histories still recall how Mkwawa, the leader of the Hehe people, attacked columns of German troops and raided German military outposts in the southern part of the country from 1891 until his death in 1898.

The fierceness and brutality of the German military campaign were accompanied by natural disasters that greatly damaged the region's economy. Locust plagues throughout the 1890s destroyed farm crops and led to widespread famine. At the same time, rinderpest, a fatal viral disease that spreads rapidly through animals, infected the cattle herds, sometimes killing all the cattle in a village.

The Germans ruled Tanzania by dividing it into 22 administrative districts or regions. A German official responsible to the colony's governor was put in charge of each district; because of poor communications with

The Germans divided Tanzania into 22 administrative districts. Each was headed by a German official responsible to the governor, whose residence is shown here.

the capital, he was usually the final judge of how the district should be ruled. The district official often delegated authority to an *akida*, an agent (usually Arab or Swahili) who carried out the district official's orders. With the aid of Christian missionaries, schools were built and black Africans were encouraged to attend and learn to read and write in Swahili. Other schools taught vocational skills, such as carpentry.

German rule brought immense economic changes to Tanzania. The slave trade was finally brought to an end. Germans were invited to settle in Tanzania and build coffee, cotton, and sisal plantations. Two railroad lines were built, one stretching north from the port at Tanga to Mount Kilimanjaro, the other paralleling the old caravan route from Dar es Salaam to Kigoma and Ujimi. These rail lines hastened the development of the plan-

Led by local inhabitants, the district commissioner of Pemba visits an outlying village.

tations, because they let growers send their crops quickly and easily to the harbors at Dar es Salaam and Tanga.

But the Germans did not develop Tanzania's economy for the benefit of the Tanzanians. Plantation crops were grown for the cash they earned the plantation owners. A yearly tax, called the hut tax, was levied on each dwelling in every village in the colony. The Africans were required to pay this tax in cash, which could only be obtained by working for the whites. And black Africans were forced to work on the plantations, where they earned low wages, lived in poor housing, and could be flogged for not following orders.

Hatred of the Germans was intense, and in 1905, hatred turned to revolt in the Maji Maji Rebellion. The rebellion had its roots in the German colonial authorities' decision to develop cotton plantations. Africans were forced to work the cotton fields. The first year's harvest of cotton was low, and the Africans received almost no money for their labor. Some of the cotton plantation workers had become followers of a prophet named Kinjiktile, who claimed he had a medicine, *maji*, that turned bullets into water. Emboldened by Kinjiktile's speeches and believing in the power of maji, the workers attacked and burned German military posts and farms to protest their forced labor on the cotton plantations.

The rebellion spread among workers on other plantations, and the Germans moved to crush it. German machine guns killed hundreds of Africans who attacked posts after anointing themselves with maji. German troops destroyed the crops and burned the villages of the rebellion's supporters. Still, it took almost three years for the Germans to regain control of the land. More than 250,000 Africans died in the rebellion and from the famine that spread through the land when the rebellion ended in 1908. Tanzanians today consider the Maji Maji Rebellion the first movement for independence.

World War I brought an end to German rule. Although the main battles of the war were fought in Europe, important naval and land battles also took place in the European nations' colonies. British and German gunboats fought pitched battles on the waters of Lake Victoria. British troops, including many black African askaris under the command of a South African, General Jan Smuts, moved south from what is now Kenya and forced German troops and German askaris out of the cities and villages of Tanzania. Fighting was difficult, because the Germans were experienced and had expert commanders, but by 1917 the British occupied the entire colony. The worst enemy for both sides was the environment: diseases such as dysentery and malaria killed thousands of soldiers, and many others were killed by lions and rhinoceroses.

British Rule

At the end of the war in 1918, the League of Nations (the forerunner of today's United Nations) granted Britain a mandate to "administer" the former German territory. The mandate gave Britain full responsibility for governing the colony and required that Britain promote the "moral well-being" of the colony's subjects. In 1922, Britain formally took control of the colony and gave it the name Tanganyika.

With the help of African askaris like these, the British drove the Germans out of Tanzania during World War I.

The first few years of British rule were benevolent. German plantations were sold, often to British citizens, but many went to Indians, who had begun to migrate to the colony in increasing numbers. Black Tanganyikans were encouraged to grow cash crops (crops that were sold for money) such as coffee. Many found coffee production profitable, and it became the country's most popular crop for farmers with small plots of land.

Black Tanganyikans also began to work on the plantations the British and the Indians had purchased. Working conditions were much better than under German rule, because the British outlawed forced labor and floggings. The new owners cultivated sisal plants, whose fibers are used to make rope. By the 1930s, sisal was Tanganyika's most important export crop; indeed, Tanganyika supplied 36 percent of the world's supply of sisal by 1938.

But the Great Depression of 1929—which affected almost every country in the world—sharply reduced the prices Tanganyika received for its coffee and sisal. This meant that farmers and workers received lower wages. The Tanganyikan economy recovered somewhat after the depression, but World War II and the years after the war did nothing to invigorate the economy. In short, as one leading historian of Tanganyika put it, "continuing poverty was the leading characteristic [of Tanganyika] under British rule."

Britain's political administration of Tanganyika was much more constructive than its economic administration. In 1925, the second British governor of Tanganyika, Sir Donald Cameron, arrived in Dar es Salaam from Nigeria, where he had promoted the idea of indirect rule. He introduced the same idea of indirect rule into Tanganyika. Under this system, the colony's people were responsible for day-to-day local government, including running the court system and the treasury; the British provided guidance and government at the federal, or national, level.

The British divided Tanganyika into 11 provinces. Within each province, the British approved "chiefs" who were to govern their "tribes."

Smaller "tribes" were governed by the "chiefs" of larger "tribes." Many of the Tanganyikan people, however, did not consider themselves to be members of tribes, and as a result they did not have traditional chiefs for rulers. The British created artificial tribal identities for such people and then supervised the selection of chiefs for them.

Governor Cameron also introduced a Legislative Council, which was made up of British and Indians who were nominated by the governor. No Africans or Arabs were represented on the Council, which gave advice to the governor on ruling the country. Cameron believed that the Africans needed time to learn how to govern themselves locally before they could govern at a higher level.

Because Cameron believed in educating the Africans to rule themselves, the British turned their attention to improving education. Many of the graduates of the school system became civil servants—employees of the British government who served as administrators and clerks. These British-educated civil servants and other educated Africans were intended to become the colony's future leaders. But they became leaders more quickly than the British wished—by creating a movement to make Tanganyika an independent nation.

In the 1890s, the British ended slavery on Zanzibar. The island's British administrator lived in this official dwelling, which was called a residency.

Two Independent Nations

The British did not lavish attention and money on Tanganyika and Zanzibar, because they did not consider them as important as their other colonies scattered throughout the world. This inattention may have benefited Tanganyika and Zanzibar in the long run, because it allowed them to achieve independence without fighting a war with Great Britain.

The British continued their policy of indirect rule in Tanganyika until after World War II. During the war, more than 80,000 Tanganyikans fought with the British. In 1946, the United Nations changed the terms of Britain's mandate for Tanganyika. The territory officially became a Trust Territory of Britain, and Britain was told to prepare Tanganyika for independence.

The British worked to follow this new mandate. Building on the system of indirect rule, the British had already allowed two Africans to sit on the Legislative Council in 1945; by 1949, two more had joined. However, the Africans were considered "unofficial" members. They could not vote, so they actually had little political power.

The United Nations sent two fact-finding committees to Tanganyika, and they reported that these unofficial seats on the Council could not be considered real progress toward independence. In response, the British governor of Tanganyika, Sir Edward Twining, proposed a program that would give political representation to Africans as well as to the European and Asian settlers in Tanganyika. Under Twining's proposal, people from all three races would be elected or chosen to sit on local and county councils.

This approach pleased the British and the Asians, but the Africans rejected it, because it did not recognize them as the majority. Many Africans did not want a share in a multiracial government; they wanted a black African government. The feeling that Tanganyika should have an independent African identity gave rise to a nationalist movement, which created the Tanganyika African Association (TAA) in 1929. The TAA brought together civil servants and urban leaders from Dar es Salaam to express African opinions on unity and independence.

The TAA held its first territorial conference in 1940. TAA members passed a resolution asking the British government to form governing boards on which Africans could sit. The TAA conference in 1945 decided that it was necessary to organize the Tanganyikan people by having a branch of the TAA in the chief town of each province.

During the 1940s and the 1950s, several grievances fueled nationalist feeling among black Tanganyikans. Blacks were afraid that their land would be taken from them by the government. They resented legislation that made them grow crops chosen by the British to aid agricultural development. This resentment caused the TAA to change into the Tanganyika African National Union (TANU) in 1954.

The differences between TAA and TANU were large. TAA had been partly social, partly political. TANU was a political organization with a single goal: *uhuru*, or independence. TANU gave new life to the black nationalist movement. It took advantage of the people's discontent and encouraged farmers to enroll as members of TANU. As a result, whenever disturbances occurred, the government blamed TANU.

TANU's success with the farmers and its forceful yet peaceful calls for independence were the handiwork of Julius Nyerere, TANU's first presi-

(continued on page 57)

SCENES OF
TANZANIA

◄50►

➤ *Masai men must jump their own heights in their traditional jump-dancing.*

◄

Giraffes, the national animals of Tanzania, are hunted for their meat, hides, and tails.

▼ *Tanzanians gather at a roadside market in Dar es Salaam.*

▲ *Lake Victoria, in northwest Tanzania, is Africa's largest lake. Much of the land around the lake is used for farming, and the lake itself is heavily fished.*

▲ *This ambling zebra is one of thousands that inhabit Tanzania's wildlife preserves.*

◄ *These Masai children are gathering water.*

➤ *Mount Kilimanjaro in Tanzania is Africa's highest mountain. Despite lying near the equator, it is snow-capped.*

▲ *This full-grown male lion rests on the Serengeti Plain, Tanzania's most famous wildlife preserve.*

➤ *Zanzibar's picturesque old town is a historic port city.*

◄

This Masai warrior wears a traditional headdress and paint.

⋀ *Dhows (sailing ships of Arab design) in Zanzibar harbor are an important means of carrying goods.*

▲ About 44 percent of the
population is Christian.
This rural church is near
Karatu.

➤

One of Tanzania's native
plants is the treelike
candelabra cactus.

(continued from page 48)

dent. Nyerere had been a schoolteacher and one of the first black Tangan-yikans to receive his college education in Britain and the United States. Nyerere's charisma—and his belief that TANU must embrace all the peo-ple, not just the educated—forged the independence movement into a force that included all black Tanganyikans.

At first, Nyerere believed that Tanganyika could achieve indepen-dence with the help of the United Nations, but after two visits to the UN in 1955 and 1956, he realized that he would have to make many changes at home before the UN could help.

The British administration reacted to TANU's demand for an inde-pendent country ruled by the African majority. First, it changed the colo-ny's constitution. Starting in 1958, the members of the Legislative Council would be elected by the people instead of being appointed by the gover-nor. Second, the British supported the formation of the United Tangan-yika party (UTP) to oppose TANU in the 1958 elections. The UTP included a number of African chiefs who were also government officials. Third, it introduced multiracial councils throughout the country. This was a very controversial step, because most of the former councils had been all African. Now they were required to have certain numbers of Europeans and Asians as members.

At the 1958 TANU annual conference, members debated whether or not to participate in the elections for the multiracial Legislative Council and other local councils. Nyerere said that they should participate. This was wise advice. In both the 1958 and the 1959 elections, TANU won overwhelming victories. The British now saw that TANU was the voice of the people. In October 1959, the governor announced that the multiracial requirements for the councils would be eliminated. The British also moved the next elections up from 1962 to 1960.

In 1960, TANU won all but one of the seats on the Legislative Coun-cil. Nyerere was asked to become the country's first chief minister and to form his own government. The new Legislative Council included 52 Africans, 16 Europeans, 11 Asians, 1 Arab, and 1 Goan. This proved that the government could be multiracial without official regulations on Council membership.

In March 1961, the British agreed to give Nyerere's government full control of Tanganyika's domestic government by May. The British would continue to handle defense and foreign affairs. Full independence would

come in December. In May, Nyerere became the first prime minister and his Council of Ministers became the Cabinet. On December 9, 1961, Tanganyika became an independent country within the Commonwealth of Nations, an association of Great Britain and many former British colonies, bound together by trade and defense treaties. The new nation changed its name to Tanzania.

In 1891, the British protected the Sultan of Zanzibar, who lived in this palace, from the Germans.

Independent Zanzibar

While Tanganyika was moving toward independence, Zanzibar also grew impatient with colonial rule. The German colonization of Tanganyika in 1891 threatened the power of the sultan of Zanzibar. The Germans forced the sultan to give up his claims to the coast of Tanganyika. He was determined, however, not to give up his rule of Zanzibar, so he turned to the British for help. The British, who also felt threatened by the Germans' actions, declared Zanzibar a protectorate. Officially, the sultan remained in charge, but the British took over the actual administration of the island. The sultan soon discovered that his allies against the Germans had ideas of their own—and military force to back them up.

The British immediately demanded changes on Zanzibar. First, they ordered that slavery be abolished. They then reorganized the customs administration, which was Zanzibar's biggest source of funds. Taxes paid by merchants trading at Zanzibar were increased. This increase caused many merchants to leave Zanzibar for coastal ports on the mainland, so the British changed their strategy and made Zanzibar a duty-free port in February 1892.

In March 1926, the British introduced a Legislative Council. All of the council members were appointed by the British. Most important, they all came from the Arab aristocracy and the Indian and European communities. African residents were excluded. Not until 1946 was an African appointed to the Legislative Council.

By the mid-1950s, Zanzibarians began to call for independence from Britain. After the British announced that elections for the Legislative Council would be held in September 1957, several political parties began to form. Zanzibari Arabs formed the Zanzibar Nationalist party (ZNP) and made "Freedom Now" their motto. The Zanzibar and Pemba Peoples party (ZPPP) was formed on Pemba Island, but it eventually aligned itself with the ZNP. The African Association party was based on the same principles as TANU on the mainland. The Shirazi (mixed African-Arab) people of Zanzibar joined with the African Association to form the Afro-Shirazi

Union (ASU), because they feared an Arab victory in upcoming elections. The ASU was formed with the help of Tanganyikan leader Nyerere. The party changed its name to the Afro-Shirazi party (ASP) in 1957.

In September 1957, the first general elections to the Legislative Council occurred in Zanzibar. The ASP received more than 60 percent of the votes on Zanzibar, but its poor showing on Pemba reduced its overall total to about 40 percent. (The ZPPP received the largest number of votes on Pemba.) Thus, the ZNP won the largest number of seats.

The ZNP was again the victor in 1961, winning 13 of the 23 seats on the Council. But conflict developed on Zanzibar between the ZNP and the ASP. The ZNP (mostly Arabs) stressed Zanzibarian nationalism, while the ASP wanted Zanzibar to become part of the black African community on the mainland.

In the midst of this unrest, the British decided to grant Zanzibar and Pemba internal self-government in June 1963. In July 1963, the ZNP and the ZPPP again triumphed and won 18 of the 31 seats on the Legislative Council. However, the ASP won a large percentage of the popular vote. The two islands became completely independent in December 1963, but many black citizens called it "Uhuru wa Waarabu," or "Arab independence" because of the ZNP majority in the government. Thus, independence did not bring an end to unrest on the islands.

Julius Nyerere was prime minister when independence was declared in 1962. He resigned in 1962 but was later elected president again.

The United Republic

During the first three years of Tanzania's independence, the country's leaders reorganized the government along socialist lines. First, local government offices were placed under the direct control of the central government. All land was declared government property; existing claims to land were made into long-term leases, so that landowners became tenants on state land. Finally, a unified system of laws was written and a judicial system was established.

Julius Nyerere was prime minister when independence was declared, but early in 1962 he told the astonished people that he was resigning. Nyerere said he planned to study how best the Tanzanian African National Union (TANU) should rule Tanzania. One of his ideas was that only one party should rule Tanzania. Nyerere thought one-party rule strengthened democracy because it gave people a better opportunity to choose their leaders than when two or more parties competed for support.

Rashidi Kawawa, a TANU leader who took Nyerere's place when he resigned, kept Nyerere's Cabinet and announced that Nyerere was still the "Father of the Country." However, Nyerere decided to return to public life when the government declared Tanzania a republic on December 9, 1962. In elections held afterward, Nyerere won the new position of president by receiving more than 98 percent of the 1,100,000 votes cast.

One of the first problems Nyerere encountered as president was a conflict between the government and the labor unions. The unions had forced wages up so fast that employers had been unable to keep many workers in their jobs. Relations between the government and the unions became strained. In 1964, some union leaders helped military officers attempt a coup (a forcible takeover of the government). The government defeated the coup attempt and used the opportunity to take away the unions' power. It created one union organization, the National Union of Tanganyika Workers. The government named the union's officials and controlled its finances.

Zanzibar Joins the Mainland

In April 1964, President Nyerere of Tanzania and President Abeid Karume of Zanzibar agreed to unite their countries because of their shared history and geographic closeness. President Karume's decision to unite Zanzibar with the mainland followed two tumultuous years of violence. At independence in 1963, the new Arab government on Zanzibar had made several mistakes that angered the African majority and resulted in revolution. First, the government set agricultural policies that benefited the plantation owners, who were mainly Arabs. Second, the government ignored the fact that its main supporters were located on Pemba Island or in the rural regions of Zanzibar. Most Africans on Zanzibar did not support the government. However, its worst mistake was reorganizing the police force. The government removed most of the experienced African and European police officers and replaced them with government supporters who were not experienced. Many of the police officers who had been fired joined an antigovernment revolutionary movement.

A 250-member revolutionary force attacked on the morning of January 12, 1964, and gained control of the capital city of Zanzibar by the afternoon. The revolutionary force, led by John Okello, came from the Zanzibar and Pemba Peanut Workers Union, the Afro-Shirazi Youth League, and the former African policemen. The rebels took control of the

President Abeid Karume of Zanzibar united his country with Tanzania to form the United Republic of Tanzania.

government. They appointed a Revolutionary Council to govern the island. Riots broke out on Zanzibar and more than 5,000 Arabs were killed. Another 5,000 Arabs went into exile. Within weeks, the revolutionaries forced Okello out of power and made Abeid Karume president of the revolutionary government. Zanzibar and Pemba were now called the People's Republic of Zanzibar and Pemba.

Tanzania's president Nyerere liked Karume's policies. He suggested a union between the two countries. When they joined in April of 1964, they took the name the United Republic of Tanzania. Nyerere was president; Karume was vice president and also president of Zanzibar. Nyerere also replaced three of his ministers with Zanzibaris. In spite of the union, however, the mainland and Zanzibar have kept their own separate methods of government. Today Zanzibar still has its own president, who is chosen in separate elections.

The mainland government wanted both political and economic development to follow African traditions. It believed that a one-party state and control of the trade union movement were the first steps in this direction. Over the next few years, the government also made several changes to benefit the people, including laws governing the minimum wage, severance pay, and social security benefits.

The most significant government act was the Arusha Declaration, which was announced in February 1967. The Arusha Declaration outlined how the social and economic development of Tanzania would take place through socialism and self-reliance. Socialism was defined as: equal opportunity to work; government ownership and control of the economy; and democratic government through popular vote. Self-reliance was defined as: hard and intelligent work by the people, especially in agriculture; and not taking grants, loans, or foreign investments to develop the country.

While the Arusha Declaration and other changes on the mainland seemed to be in the best interests of the people, changes on Zanzibar did not benefit the population. The mainland had wanted a union with Zanzibar in order to encourage democracy on the island. However, Karume, the head of the Zanzibarian government, did not want democracy. Karume's government took over the island's radio station and newspapers and used them for propaganda (information that supports and glorifies the government). Western publications were censored and sometimes banned. The government closely watched everyone who entered the country, especially journalists. Political lectures supporting the government became part of the school program.

By 1970, the economy of Zanzibar, except for clove exports, had collapsed. The collapse was brought about by poor planning, a shortage of skilled workers, and bad government management of nationalized businesses (companies or services taken over by the government). The most serious economic problem was the shortage of food. Since 1964, the government had controlled food imports and had closed down many food shops. Karume wanted Zanzibar to be self-sufficient at any cost. For example, he wanted the people to stop eating bread, because the island's climate did not allow the growing of wheat.

On April 7, 1972, Karume was assassinated by a soldier who believed Karume had betrayed the revolution. Karume's murder threw the government into a state of confusion.

A new leader, Aboud Jumbe, quickly eliminated some of Karume's policies. He allowed food imports and permitted the purchase of foreign materials urgently needed for economic development. Jumbe encouraged good relations with the mainland. Political and military ties were strengthened. In 1977, the islands' ruling African-Shirazi party and the mainland's Tanzanian African National Union merged to form the new Revolutionary party of Tanzania, or Chama Cha Mapinduzi in Swahili. The Revolutionary party (CCM) became the only legal party in Tanzania. It was responsible for all political activity and state functions.

For the next few years, Tanzania concentrated on strengthening its economy and helping other African peoples achieve freedom. For example, in early 1973, President Nyerere allowed refugees from ethnic conflicts in

Ali Hassan Mwinyi was elected president and successor to Nyerere in 1985.

Burundi to enter Tanzania. Another example of Tanzania's international action concerns Uganda. In February 1973, General Idi Amin, the dictator of Uganda, accused Tanzania of plotting to remove him from power. Relations between Uganda and Tanzania remained poor until October 1978, when fighting broke out between the two countries. One month later Uganda claimed the Kagera Salient, a slice of land that included about 708 square miles (1840 sq km) of Tanzanian territory.

The Organization of African Unity (OAU) asked Uganda to withdraw its troops. Uganda agreed, but border fighting continued. In January 1979, an army made up of 20,000 members of the Tanzanian People's Defense Forces and 1,200 Ugandan exiles invaded Uganda. By April, the invasion force had gained control of the country. Amin fled the country. Tanzanian troops remained in Uganda while national elections were held for a new government.

Tanzania also aided Africans who demanded change in white-ruled Southern Rhodesia (now Zimbabwe). Tanzania supported the Patriotic Front led by Zimbabwean guerrillas Joshua Nkomo and Robert Mugabe from January 1977 until April 1980, when Zimbabwe became an independent, African-ruled state.

In early 1984, a political crisis developed on Zanzibar. Aboud Jumbe, the president of Zanzibar, and three of his ministers resigned because they disagreed with the mainland's policies toward Zanzibar. In April, Ali Hassan Mwinyi, a former schoolteacher and supporter of the union between Zanzibar and the mainland, was elected president of the island. President Mwinyi calmed tensions between the mainland and Zanzibar.

On November 5, 1985, elections were held for president of Tanzania. Nyerere, who had held the post since independence, had announced that he was retiring and would no longer serve as president. Mwinyi won the election and became the first Zanzibarian to govern both Zanzibar and the mainland. Another first was the fact that Nyerere turned over power peacefully to Mwinyi—in many other African countries, changes in leadership have often been violent. The peaceful change of presidents was a tribute to Nyerere's skill and leadership.

The change in the presidency initiated a change in social policy. In 1986, the Mwinyi government adopted a market-oriented economic strategy that included a number of reform measures. The new strategy encouraged private enterprise and reduced government planning and regulation. It was adopted under pressure from the World Bank, the International Monetary Fund, and other international organizations that provided Tanzania with assistance. In spite of all Nyerere's hopes, the economy had been stagnating and Tanzania's international debt had been steadily increasing.

In 1992, the political system was reformed, too. The United Republic's constitution was amended and political parties became legal. In 1995, for the first time in its history, Tanzania held a multiparty election. The CCM candidate for president, Benjamin Mkapa, was opposed by candidates from three other parties. Mkapa received 61.8 percent of the vote, and the second-place candidate, Augustine Mrema, received 27.8 percent. In the parliamentary election, the CCM ended up with 186 of the 232 elected seats in the parliament. The other seats were divided among four opposition parties.

Makombe tribesmen, such as this man from neighboring Mozambique, often work in Tanzania because of their skill as sisal cutters.

The Tanzanian People

The nation of Tanzania is made up of Africans, Asians, Arabs, and Europeans, with most people on the mainland Africans, who belong to more than 130 different ethnic groups. The north-central section of the mainland has four major peoples: the Khoisan, Cushitic, Bantus, and Nilotes. The Khoisan, the original inhabitants of Tanzania, have almost disappeared through intermarriage with other ethnic groups. The Cushites, the first farmers of Tanzania, originally came from the Ethiopian highlands. The Bantu are the largest family of ethnic groups in Tanzania. The most numerous Bantu groups today are the Sukuma and the Nyamwezi. The Nilotes, the last large group to migrate to Tanzania, are divided into three branches: the Tatoga, the Masai, and the Luo.

On the southern slopes of Mount Kilimanjaro live the Chagga, one of the largest ethnic groups in Tanzania. In 1995, they numbered more than 1 million. The Chagga, an industrious and resourceful people, have become wealthy because of the coffee they produce. Their well-developed irrigation system brings water over long distances to each homestead, making it a lush garden. A single family occupies a homestead, which is usually enclosed by a high hedge. Within the hedge is a house and a garden. In the past, Chagga houses were shaped like beehives, with roofs made from thatched banana leaves or grass. Today, bricks, blocks, and corrugated steel sheets are used. Cattle and goats are kept in their own section of the homestead. The house has a reception room, various storage areas for food and tools, bedrooms, and a hearth.

One of the traditional rites still observed by the Chagga is circumcision. It is performed during adolescence on both boys and girls. The circumcision is followed by instruction in the responsibilities and rights of an adult. Circumcision is considered necessary for a man to receive his inheritance and his political rights, and for a woman to sell the produce from her fields or to bear children.

The Masai are a small but significant group that has held firmly to its traditions. They are divided into two groups: the Arusha, who are the agricultural, or farming, Masai; and the pastoral Masai, who are nomads. The pastoral Masai roam free with their cattle herds. Most of their villages are semipermanent—they are moved every three or four years with the cattle. When a village is set up, its small rectangular huts are arranged in a circle. A thorn fence is built to surround the village to protect the cattle, sheep, and goats from predators. Several families live in a village. Each village family owns a herd, but all the animals are kept together and tended by the sons of the families.

Masai society is organized by age. Each age-set, or group of people in a given age bracket, has specific responsibilities and privileges. Members of the same age-set (usually a span of 10 to 20 years) are expected to regard each other as family members. Every adult Masai male belongs to an age-set. When he is circumcised at the age of 16, he joins the age grade of *ilmurran*, or *moran*. He remains a moran for seven to fourteen years. At the end of this period, all moran are simultaneously promoted to the status of elders. For the first time they are allowed to take snuff, chew tobacco, and raise a family. In the past, the moran acted as the Masai army, responsible for defending Masai territory. Today they help with difficult work, such as moving herds to a new pasture during a drought.

Women are circumcised at the beginning of puberty. They may not marry until they have been circumcised. The Masai do not limit the num-

Two Masai tend one of their cattle, which shows signs of suffering from the drought that has often plagued Masailand.

ber of wives a man may have. However, the husband must have enough cattle to provide enough milk for each wife and her children, because cow's milk is the staple food of the Masai.

The Masai believe in one god, who is called Ngai. Ngai is also the Masai word for sky and air. Ngai is responsible for everything that happens in the world. He automatically punishes those who commit certain sins, such as killing a helpless animal. Most Masai religious ceremonies celebrate a person's passage through the various stages of life. Death, however, is not recognized; the Masai do not believe in an afterlife. The death of all but the oldest village member is ignored out of respect for the feelings of the dead person's family.

The Africans of Zanzibar divide themselves into two groups: Africans from the mainland and Shirazis. The mainland Africans are considered the "lower" class, because their ancestors were brought to Zanzibar as slaves. The Shirazi are descendants of the original African inhabitants of Zanzibar who intermarried with colonists from Persia (now Iran). They are called Shirazi because the Persians came from a town called Shiraz.

The Asians on the mainland and on Zanzibar are the Indian and Pakistani descendants of traders who emigrated to Tanzania generations ago. The Indians are the leading businessmen in Tanzania.

The Europeans—especially the Germans and the British—came to Tanzania as colonists. Their numbers have declined since independence. However, Americans, Russians, Germans, Chinese, Italians, and Canadians have arrived to teach, organize, and build.

African prejudice against the Europeans and the Asians is a problem in Tanzania. Some Africans are especially prejudiced toward Asians, because they have well-paying jobs as skilled workers, traders, and businessmen. Although the Asians have little voice in the government, they have an important economic role in Tanzania.

The few remaining Arabs living on Zanzibar make up four distinct communities. The first group is the Shihiri. The Shihiri are mainly traders who are descended from the Shihr on the Hadhrami coast of the People's Democratic Republic of Yemen. Next are the Omani Arabs from Oman on the Persian Gulf. The Omani were the landowners and the ruling elite until the revolution. The third group are the descendants of Arabs who arrived long before the Portuguese came to East Africa. This group includes the Mazrui clan, who were related to members of the Yarubi dynasty, which ruled Zanzibar before the Omani Arabs came to the island. The fourth community includes the Shirazi and the Swahili (Africans and Arabs who have intermarried). Both the Shirazi and Swahili have Arab blood but are not fully accepted by other Arabs as their kinsmen.

Many of the ethnic groups in Tanzania have their own language. Fortunately, most of the people can speak Swahili, so it is the common language. Swahili is a Bantu-based language that uses many Arabic words. Unlike other Bantu languages, Swahili has long been a written language, using the Arabic alphabet. The name Swahili comes from the Arabic word *sahel*, which means "coastal dwellers." It developed as a trading language, one that could be understood by the mainland Africans and the Arab traders who set up trading posts on the Tanzanian mainland and Zanzibar. At independence, President Julius Nyerere decided that Swahili should be the national language. He argued that it was the common language in the country and was not associated with a ruling ethnic group.

Nyerere's choice of Swahili was wise, because it allowed Tanzanians to have a national language that belongs to all Tanzanians.

Modern Dress

Most Tanzanians dress today in conservative, modern clothing. Fashionable or trendy clothing is not acceptable. Extremely short, tight-fitting, or low-cut dresses are considered unsuitable for a woman. Modesty, however, is relative. Although Swahili women cover themselves from head to toe in a form of Islamic dress, the traditional dress of a married Masai woman is a brief leather skirt and many ornaments. A Masai woman would be overcome with shame if anyone, even her husband, saw her without the special brass earrings that she wears to show that she is married.

Each of the African ethnic groups has its own superstitions and beliefs. The people who live near Mount Kilimanjaro believe it is "God's throne." They believe that a man will be unable to raise children if a woman walks between him and the mountain. The Nyakusa of southern Tanzania believe it is very important to share food fairly among their neighbors. They believe that witches, roused by the smell of roasting meat, try to drive apart the neighbors gathered for a feast. The Nyakusa also believe that witches create jealousy among a man's wives.

Tanzanian women tend to dress simply and modestly.

Traditional African religions still play an important part in many Tanzanians' lives. These religions offer guidelines and instruction for everyday living. Such guidance might include information on nature: how to track animals, find one's way through the bush, or tend a farm.

Today most Tanzanians practice either Christianity or Islam, often combined with elements of traditional religions. About 44 percent are Christian and 37 percent are Muslim. Approximately 19 percent follow traditional religions only. A very small number are Hindus or Bahais. The major Christian religions practiced include Anglican, Greek Orthodox, Lutheran, and Roman Catholic.

Because of the Arab influence, Islam has spread throughout Tanzania, especially on Zanzibar. Most Muslims (followers of Islam) belong to the Sunni or Shiite sects. The Sunnis believe that the first four caliphs (or leaders) of Islam were true successors of Mohammed, the founder of the faith. The Shiites consider Ali, the Prophet Mohammed's son-in-law, the direct successor to Mohammed. Almost all the Arab and African Muslims in Tanzania are Sunnis. Most of the Indian Muslims on Zanzibar are Shiites.

The marriage traditions of the Sunnis and Shiites show the difference between the two sects. When a Sunni Muslim boy wishes to marry, he first chooses a girl. He then tells either his uncle or his grandfather, who contacts the girl's grandparents. If the grandparents are interested in the engagement of their granddaughter to the boy, they and the boy's grandparents tell the parents of the boy and the girl that they approve of the marriage. A bride-price (money to be paid to the bride's parents) is set. The groom then pays two-thirds of the bride-price to the bride's family (the rest is paid after the marriage).

Traditionally, when a Shiite Muslim boy wants to get married, he tells his parents. The parents then find a suitable girl. Once a girl is decided upon, the girl's parents examine the boy. They study his family background and his future prospects. They discuss his religious behavior with the community leaders and interview his friends. When the girl's parents say that they are satisfied with the boy, the boy's parents make a formal visit to the girl's parents and announce that their son wants to marry the daughter. If the girl's parents accept the proposal, the boy and the girl are considered engaged. The engagement can only be broken for a very good reason. The engaged couple may not see each other until their marriage, which usually occurs about a year after the engagement.

Not all Sunni Muslims marry in the traditional manner. Today, many young girls and boys tell their parents directly that they wish to marry. And although most Shiite parents still arrange their children's marriages, the engaged couples are often allowed to see each other during the engagement. These changes have occurred because of the government's attempt to make men and women equal in education and job opportunities.

The traditional religious and ethnic practices of most Tanzanian cultures discriminated against women. Since independence, however, the government has encouraged women to work outside their homes. Women now meet young men either at work or at informal gatherings, where they are no longer sexually segregated. Also, Tanzanians are marrying later. Today, the average age of marriage for women is 19. The average age at which women have their first child is 20.

The lifestyle of the Tanzanian woman has changed dramatically since the mid-1950s. Before then, the typical Tanzanian woman was a modest, quiet person who carried a bundle balanced on her head and a baby on her back. She was regarded as a household possession, who could be bought as part of a marriage transaction. But when TANU started organizing an independence movement, women were urged to join. They formed committees and sponsored fund-raising projects. By 1965, there were seven women in the National Assembly. Three of them were junior members of President Nyerere's cabinet.

Life in Tanzania

Most Tanzanians are peasant farmers or nomads like the Masai. They produce barely enough food to survive. In 1995, the gross domestic product per person was only $900. (Gross domestic product is the total value of all

*Most Tanzanian children
receive some primary
education.*

the goods and services produced in a country.) To improve the life of the average Tanzanian, the government introduced universal free primary education in 1977. The government believed that education would make the people more willing to use modern methods of farming and livestock care, which in turn would raise the standard of living. Seventy percent of Tanzanian children now receive primary education. The adult literacy rate (the percentage of adults who can read and write) increased from 33 percent in 1967 to 68 percent by the mid-1990s.

Money shortage affects the diet of the average Tanzanian. Meals are usually one-pot dishes, because this type of cooking can stretch a small amount of food among many people. Spiced meat (when available) and vegetables are served with filling grains and bread, rice, or stiff porridge. Because meat is a luxury, Tanzanian cooks have developed creative recipes for meats such as traditional lamb and beef as well as camel and wildebeest. Most Tanzanians get their protein from combining grains and beans or peas instead of from meat. Grain-and-legume combinations include rice and beans, beans and corn, lentils and millet, or peas and wheat.

Some traditional Tanzanian dishes are futari, which uses a mixture of coconut, citrus, cinnamon and cloves to season pumpkin or winter squash; eggplant curry; fried cabbage, which combines cabbage with carrots, tomatoes, and bell peppers seasoned with curry; potato balls, which are made with lime juice, chili peppers, chickpea flour, and coconuts; and beans with shredded coconut, garlic, cumin, coriander, lime, turmeric, and chili peppers.

Tanzanians who live on the coast, on the islands, or near the many lakes have made fish an important part of their diet. Fish is used in soups and stews, made into flavorful sauces, or simply grilled with butter. Tanzanians do not usually eat desserts that are baked or made with sugar. The typical ending to an African meal is a piece of fresh fruit.

Water is the primary drink in Tanzania and the rest of Africa, but it is often in short supply during a drought. Tanzanians also turn local plants into slightly fermented beverages such as fruit ciders, palm wines, and honey beers. Milk is drunk when available.

Tanzanians enjoy several sports. Hunting game is popular with both Tanzanians and tourists. In fact, game-hunting safaris are a carefully regulated tourist attraction. Some of the game animals hunted include elephant, buffalo, antelope, giraffe, hippopotamus, zebra, lion, and leopard.

In the Morogoro region, a Tanzanian makes sorghum beer (fermented from a grain called sorghum) outside his house.

Most game animals can be used for food, although they are usually hunted for their skins or, in the case of the elephants, their tusks. Giraffes are sought for their meat and hides, as well as for their tails, which are used as fly whisks or made into women's bracelets. Several types of birds are also hunted, including guinea fowl, francolin (a type of partridge), duck, geese, and quail.

The waters off the coast of Tanzania attract sport fisherman from around the world. Dolphin, horse mackerel, sailfish, and rock cod are just a few of the big fish that inhabit the Indian Ocean waters. Tanzania's lakes also offer good fishing. Lake Tanganyika, the second deepest lake in the world, contains more than 200 varieties of fish, some of which weigh 100 pounds (45 kilograms) or more.

Mountain climbing is another popular sport. Mount Kilimanjaro is an attractive climb for both the experienced and the amateur climber. Climbing Mount Meru is strenuous but is not difficult or dangerous.

Tanzanians who live near the coast and the lakes enjoy swimming. Most ocean beaches are easily accessible from the road. Tanzanians usually wear sneakers when swimming because the ocean floor is very rocky near the coast.

Cities and Towns

Tanzania is one of the less urbanized countries in the world—only 23 percent of its population lives in urban areas. The capital, Dar es Salaam, is the largest city, with 2 million inhabitants. Tanzania's other sizable cities include Mwanza, with 225,000 inhabitants; Dodoma (the future capital), with 200,000; Tanga, with 190,000; Zanzibar city, with 160,000; and Arusha, with 140,000.

Dar es Salaam became the capital because of its location on the coast. Its location also made it the trade and industrial center of the country. Like Dar es Salaam, the harbor cities of Tanga in the north and Mtara in

A policewoman indicates to voters where the nearest polling place is in Dar Es Salaam. Although Tanzania as a whole is rural, Dar Es Salaam is a city with 2 million inhabitants.

the south also developed into trade centers. Because Tanga is located near the fertile lands at the foot of Mount Kilimanjaro, it has become the site for agricultural exports.

After independence, the government decided to make Dodoma, which is located almost directly in the center of Tanzania, the country's future capital. Some government administrative functions have been moved there, and the city is also attracting foreign businesses that have to deal with the government. The government wants to move all remaining governmental activities to Dodoma soon. It also plans to build an international airport to serve the new capital.

The city of Zanzibar, the seat of government on Zanzibar Island, is built on a one-and-a-half-mile (2.4-km) long triangular peninsula. It has two main sections: Stone Town, which houses the island government, and the inner town, known as Ngambo.

Tanzania has always been a rural society, because the majority of Tanzanians make their living by subsistence farming. After independence, the government encouraged industrialization and education. This caused many people to leave rural areas for the towns. There were not enough jobs for the new town dwellers, however, and unemployment rose.

To stop the movement to the towns, the government created *ujamaa* (togetherness) villages. Nyerere believed that the ujamaa villages would allow the rural population to live and work together for the good of all. These villages would bring the scattered rural population together, increase agricultural production, allow the introduction of new technology, increase farmers' income, provide better social services to the people, and encourage self-reliance. The government began the ujamaa village policy in the 1960s. By 1977, a great number of rural Tanzanians lived in villages instead of in scattered homesteads.

The results of the ujamaa policy were uneven. Millions of rural Tanzanians were forced to move to the ujamaa villages. Many did not like the idea of communal (group) farming—in fact, in most areas ujamaa villagers farmed their own individual plots of land. Harvests were lower than expected. However, other village enterprises were more successful. Villagers joined together to build schools, medical clinics, water-supply facilities, and shops.

Arts and Culture

According to a Tanzanian commissioner of culture, an African's culture includes the food he eats, the clothes he wears, and the house in which he lives. The arts in Tanzania reflect this view. Aspects of everyday life, including music, dance, baskets, pottery, calabash work, jewelry, ornamental weapons, decorated furniture and household items, body painting, and scarification (ornamental scars), are all considered art forms.

Ethnic groups throughout Tanzania use music and dance in ceremonies to mark a successful hunt or to ensure fertility and good crops. Traditional music is closely tied to the local language, so that each people has a music unique to its language. In traditional music, melody is not as important as the sound and rhythm of the words. In addition to traditional music, Tanzania also has modern or popular music. In the towns, bands play Latin American and jazz music. Many young singers compose and perform ballads on the guitar. Some of these songs express political views.

Woodcarvings are the major form of art produced in Tanzania. The Chagga people, who live at the base of Mount Kilimanjaro, have always carved their household utensils from wood. Their household items are decorated with various designs, such as the sun and moon, and with animals, weapons, and huntsmen.

The Makonde of southern Tanzania are known for their animal statuettes, carved ancestor figures, ceremonial masks representing human faces, and figurines of evil spirits, which are shown with long horns and massive beards. The Makonde also cicatrize (scar) their bodies from forehead to thigh. This art form looks similar to tattooing, but it uses a different process. Tattooing is done by injecting pigment under the skin; cicatrizing is done by cutting the flesh, rubbing charcoal in the wound, and allowing it to heal over to form a black scar. Both men and women are cicatrized. Many young people now refuse to be cicatrized because they believe it will make it more difficult to get a job.

The Swahili artists of Zanzibar are famous for their beautifully carved doors and chests, their decorated household items made of wood or metal, and their jewelry. They are also known for their musical instruments, such as the siwa, which is made of brass, ivory, or carved cowhorn.

Storytelling continues to be part of Tanzanian life. Because Swahili was the only written language for many years, almost all stories were oral folk tales. Today, a body of written Tanzanian stories exists. Many deal with the conflicts Africans feel toward the modern world. For example, P.W. Songa's short story "The Intruder" is about an African stranger from

The artists of Tanzania are famous for their beautifully carved household items, such as this rhinoceros-styled headrest.

Dar es Salaam who goes to a Masai region. He hopes to transform the region into a modern town, but he meets two young Masai men who have lived as their ancestors did and are uneducated in modern ways. The meeting makes the townsman reconsider his plans. Finally, though, he decides that life cannot stand still. People must learn to accept modern ways of living. Perhaps this story represents Tanzania's struggle to become part of the modern world without forgetting its special cultures and traditions.

Most of Tanzania's educational buildings, including this library on the Morogoro College campus, have been built with foreign aid.

Government and Social Services

When Tanzania and Zanzibar formed the United Republic of Tanzania in 1964, the leaders of both countries agreed that Zanzibar would maintain control over its local affairs. The national government based on the mainland would control foreign affairs, trade, taxation, citizenship, and immigration. This system remains in effect today. The two different members of the republic are committed to making the union work while they continue to govern themselves independently.

The government of the United Republic of Tanzania is made up of a president, his cabinet, and a parliament, which is called the National Assembly. The president, who governs both the mainland and Zanzibar, is the head of state, head of government, and commander in chief of the armed forces. The president cannot make laws on his own, but a bill passed by the National Assembly cannot become law unless he signs it.

The president appoints two vice presidents to assist him. The two vice presidents are chosen from the elected members of the National Assembly. If the president comes from the mainland, the first vice president must come from Zanzibar. If the president comes from Zanzibar, as Mwinyi did, then the first vice president must come from the mainland. The second vice president acts as the prime minister in the cabinet. The cabinet is made up of the two vice presidents and several ministers, such as the

This young mother is being tested for literacy before beginning her studies to become a secondary-school science teacher.

minister of foreign affairs and the minister of finance. The president is in charge of the cabinet.

The National Assembly of the United Republic of Tanzania makes and passes all legislation. (However, the government of Zanzibar passes legislation on most domestic affairs in Zanzibar.) Most of the members of the National Assembly are elected by all adult Tanzanians to serve for five years; but some members are appointed by the president, and others hold seats that are reserved, by law, for specific officials. The president can call for early elections. The total number of representatives in the National Assembly has changed over the years because of changes in the electoral law. In the late 1990s, there were 274 seats in the National Assembly, and 232 of the members were elected. Of the elected members, 186 belonged to the CCM, and 46 belonged to other parties.

The judicial systems of the mainland and Zanzibar differ. The judicial system on the mainland is based on the British system of a judge and a jury. There are primary courts in every district, which have limited jurisdiction. A person convicted of a crime in a primary court can appeal to the district court. District courts also have limited jurisdiction, and a person found guilty in district court can appeal to the High Court, which is located in Dar es Salaam. Appeals from the High Court are made to the Court of Appeal, which is the nation's highest court. The chief justice of Tanzania and four judges of appeal sit on the court.

On Zanzibar, the government abolished the British-based judicial system in 1970. It then set up people's courts, which preside over minor criminal cases. Instead of a judge and a jury, each people's court has a magistrate, who is elected by the people, and two assistants. Originally, a Zanzibari standing trial in the people's court was not allowed to have a lawyer. However, a new constitution in 1985 changed the law to allow defense lawyers.

Education

Former president Nyerere hoped to provide education for every Tanzanian. He believed education would lay the foundation for Tanzania's future. His successors have shared his goal. Most schools receive funds from the government. Others are funded and staffed by religious missions and other voluntary agencies.

The government has encouraged villages to set up their own schools and has given them assistance to do so. The government began this program when it discovered that rural children placed in urban schools often do not want to return to their villages after their education is finished. The government hopes youths educated in their villages will stay there and use their education to make the villages better places to live.

All children must attend seven years of primary school, which is taught in Swahili. Each grade is called a "standard." English is introduced

Morogoro Agricultural College, in Central Tanzania, is one of the country's five vocational schools.

as a foreign language in Standard III. After completing Standard VII, some students go on to secondary school. Courses in secondary school are taught entirely in English, because few books have been translated into Swahili. The abrupt change from Swahili to English is difficult for many students, because most are not fluent in English.

There are six grades, or "forms," in secondary school. Form I is the first level of secondary school. However, to graduate from Form III to Form IV, students must pass a special examination. Only those who plan to attend college usually progress beyond Form III, since Forms IV through VI are college-preparation.

The amount of education a Tanzanian student receives determines what kind of job he or she will have. Students who end their schooling after Standard VII usually go back to their villages to live as farmers or fishermen. Some may stay in the city and try to find work in a factory. Those students who finish secondary school and graduate from college are sure of good jobs in government or business.

Tanzania has five vocational schools. These schools offer training in modern agricultural techniques, as well as in skilled trades such as auto mechanics, electrical work, general mechanics, and construction.

The country's main university is the University of Dar es Salaam. The university opened with a law faculty, and it now includes a science faculty, an arts faculty, and faculties of education, engineering, and management. Approximately 3,800 students were enrolled in the late 1990s.

Transportation and Communications

The Tanzania Railways Corporation is in charge of 1,616 miles (2,600 kilometers) of rail lines. The corporation also operates vessels on Lakes Victoria, Tanganyika, and Malawi. The Tanzania-Zambia Railway Authority operates the 1,156-mile (1,860-kilometer) railway that connects Dar es Salaam to New Kapiri Mposhi in the neighboring country of Zambia.

Opened in October 1975, this line was built with technical and financial assistance from the People's Republic of China.

Tanzania has about 34,500 miles (55,600 kilometers) of roads, of which 12,700 miles (20,500 kilometers) are paved. Thirty miles (50 kilometers) are expressways. In 1991, the World Bank began coordinating a ten-year Integrated Roads Program, with the goal of upgrading 70 percent of Tanzania's trunk roads and constructing over 1,750 miles (2,800 kilometers) of new roads and more than 200 bridges. Funded by international donors, the program had a total estimated cost of $650 million.

Tanzania's many lakes have ferry and steamer service that connects the country with Kenya, Uganda, Congo, Burundi, Zambia, and Malawi. Tanzania and Burundi formed a joint shipping company in 1976; the company operates a steamer service on Lake Tanganyika.

Three major harbors are located on Tanzania's Indian Ocean coast. The harbor at Dar es Salaam contains 11 deep-water berths at which large freighters can dock, one oil jetty for small oil tankers, and offshore mooring for supertankers. Mtwara's harbor has two deep-water berths. The harbor at Tanga requires ships to anchor offshore. Large, flat-bottomed barges are then used to load and unload the ships. The Tanzania Coastal Shipping Line provides regular services to Tanzanian coastal ports, and charter services to Kenya, Mozambique, the Persian Gulf, the Indian Ocean islands, and the Middle East.

Tanzania's major international airport is at Dar es Salaam; there are also international airports at Kilimanjaro and on Zanzibar. Another international airport is planned for Dodoma, the future capital city. Air Tanzania operates domestic and international flights to Burundi, Mozambique, Rwanda, the Seychelles, Uganda, Zambia, Egypt, Greece, India, Italy, Switzerland, and Britain.

Radio, television, and the press, although they are not all directly controlled by the government, are strongly influenced by it. Most newspapers and periodicals support the government and its policies. Several newspapers and periodicals are produced regularly in Tanzania. The daily newspapers include the government-controlled *Daily News; Kipanga,* which is published on Zanzibar in Swahili; and *Uhuru,* the Swahili-language official newspaper of the CCM, the ruling party.

The only television station in Tanzania is Television Zanzibar, which broadcasts from Zanzibar. There is no television service on the mainland, but Dar es Salaam does have three radio stations. One of the stations, Radio Tanzania, is a government-owned station that broadcasts in Swahili inside Tanzania and in English to other nations. Radio Tumaini (Hope) is a Swahili station operated by the Roman Catholic Church. Its programs deal with religious, social, and economic issues. On Zanzibar, a radio station called The Voice of Zanzibar broadcasts in Swahili in three wavelengths. By the mid-1990s, according to United Nations estimates, there were 740,000 radios in Tanzania and 60,000 televisions on Zanzibar.

This rock-crusher plant provided gravel for the construction of the Tan-Zam Highway from Zambia to Dar es Salaam.

Economic Policy and Development

In 1967, the Tanzanian government issued a policy statement that became known as the Arusha Declaration (Arusha is one of Tanzania's 22 administrative regions). The Declaration stated five principles for economic and social development: (1) the government would control the economy; (2) Tanzania would become self-reliant (that is, it would not be dependent on other countries for its economic growth); (3) agriculture would be developed to provide enough food for all Tanzanians; (4) there would be social equality—for example, all people would receive similar salaries; and (5) the development of agriculture would be based on socialism (state-owned resources).

The government took several actions immediately after the declaration. Banks and most businesses were nationalized (taken over by the government). Salaries for highly paid workers were gradually lowered to close the gap between the highest paid and the lowest paid. New programs were launched to provide clean drinking water, education, and health services.

The most far-reaching change was the introduction of ujamaa villages designed for group farming. Creating ujamaa villages proved more difficult than planned, however. Most rural Tanzanians did not live in villages. Instead, they lived in traditional family homesteads scattered

throughout the countryside. At first they were asked to volunteer to join the villages. When only a few volunteered, the government began to force rural Tanzanians to move to ujamaa villages. By 1977, 11 million Tanzanians had been moved to the villages, one of the largest mass movements of people in African history.

The government's efforts in education were less disruptive and more successful. President Nyerere made education for all Tanzanians his most important goal. He believed that an educated people would be a more prosperous people. Nyerere's educational programs eventually gave Tanzania one of Africa's highest adult literacy rates.

Overall, the government's policies did not lead to a richer population, however. Tanzania remained one of the poorest countries in Africa and in the world. Agricultural yields increased but did not keep pace with the growth in population. Tanzania required increasingly larger imports of food from other countries to feed its people. The attempt to make the rest of the economy self-reliant failed, too. By the mid-1980s,

A crop-destroying pest called the large grain borer has plagued East Africa since the early 1970s. This man sprays insecticide on a village's grain store.

Fishermen bring in a day's catch at a launching stage near Mwanza, on Lake Victoria.

Tanzania needed large amounts of foreign aid to keep its economy functioning.

All through the first half of the 1980s, international organizations such as the World Bank urged Tanzania to accept major changes in its economic programs. In 1986, under President Mwinyi, the government finally reversed direction and adopted a market-oriented economic policy. The government eliminated wage and price controls and instituted other measures that reduced government control of the economy.

These changes apparently had an effect. Between 1986 and 1993, agricultural production grew 4.9 percent per year, and the rest of the economy grew at a 3.6 percent rate. Economic growth slowed by the late 1990s, but the economy still grew faster than the population. The economic growth rate averaged 2.7 percent per year, and the population growth rate had dropped to 1.5 percent.

Even today, fully 90 percent of Tanzania's work force is engaged in agriculture. Most of these people are subsistence farmers—that is, they farm to feed themselves and their families. Their basic crops include corn, cassava (a starchy root that is ground into flour), sorghum, millet, rice, wheat, and plantain (a bananalike vegetable). By the late 1990s, the gross domestic product per person in Tanzania was only $900, about one-twentieth of the gross domestic product in rich industrialized countries. Even though most of the working population is engaged in farming, Tanzania has been unable to produce enough food to feed all its people.

Like many other poor countries, Tanzania depends for its livelihood on the export of agricultural products, such as coffee, cotton, tobacco, tea, cashew nuts, and sisal. These products now account for approximately 50 percent of Tanzania's export earnings. There are signs of positive change, however. In 1988, the same group of agricultural products accounted for 80 percent of Tanzania's export income. That type of extreme dependence on a small number of products was a legacy of the colonial era. Independent Tanzania had hoped to change that legacy, and by the 1990s it was indeed making some progress.

Industry

Only 10 percent of the work force is employed in industry, and industrial production contributes only 8 percent of the nation's total domestic production (agriculture provides 58 percent). The few factories produce items for domestic use. The biggest industries are food processing, brewing, textile mills, and cement production.

Mining does not play an important role in the economy, although Tanzania has reserves of diamonds, gold, tin, coal, and iron ore. Mining adds only 1.6 percent to Tanzania's total annual production. Its share is growing, however. By the late 1990s, mining production was growing about 6 percent per year. A Canadian Company, Sutton Industries, is developing a gold deposit at Bulyanhulu that contains an estimated 3.5 million ounces (approximately $1.5 billion in U.S. currency).

Tanzania has to import most of its oil. Crude petroleum and petroleum products make up approximately 11 percent of its import bill. The country may be able to reduce its dependence on foreign oil if it takes advantage of its extensive river system to build hydroelectric power plants.

This herdsman has substituted a portable radio for the traditional herdsman's pipes. He works on a dairy farm sponsored by the United Nations.

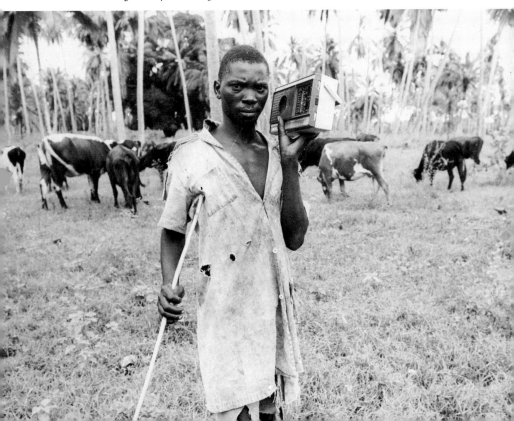

More than 70 percent of Tanzania's electricity is already generated by water power, and the government hopes to build several new dams with foreign assistance. Another hope for reducing oil imports lies in the reserves of oil and natural gas that are believed to be located near the Great Rift Valley. A Canadian company named the PetroCanada International Assistance Corporation is conducting a $27-million oil exploration program supported by the World Bank.

The Need for Foreign Aid

President Nyerere's desire to make Tanzania self-reliant has not been achieved. Today Tanzania still needs the help of other nations. Three main problems have led to Tanzania's dependence on foreign aid: low prices for Tanzania's exports; the large price increases for oil imports that took place in the 1970s; and growth in Tanzania's trade deficit (that is, Tanzania buys more items than it sells). Unable to raise enough cash from the sale of its exports, the country has asked for loans and grants to pay for the imports it needs. Over the years, many nations have responded to Tanzania's appeal. Norway, Sweden, Denmark, Germany, Great Britain, and Canada have given loans or grants. Some foreign banks have also provided Tanzania with loans.

By the late 1990s, Tanzania owed over $6.7 billion to foreign banks and international lending agencies such as the World Bank and the International Monetary Fund (IMF). Tanzania had become so dependent on foreign assistance that as much as 40 percent of its gross domestic product was based on external aid.

Social Welfare

In spite of the country's continuing economic struggles, Tanzania is justifiably proud of the improvements it has made in basic social services. Although some aspects of health care and nutrition remain poor by Western standards, they represent major achievements for a poor country.

In southern Tanzania, a pumping station provides purified water for nearby villages.

For example, because of the government's efforts, 49 percent of the population has safe drinking water. This is exactly the same as the percentage who have safe drinking water in neighboring Kenya, even though Kenya is a richer country than Tanzania, with a standard of living that is almost twice as high.

The Tanzanian government operates hospitals and health centers, and Christian missions provide additional health care. Still, a great deal remains to be done to improve the people's access to medical care. By the mid-1990s, Tanzania had one physician for every 20,511 people and one hospital bed per 1,044 people. The infant mortality rate was 106 deaths per thousand births. The life expectancy of a newborn baby was 42 years—substantially lower than in Kenya, for example, but higher than in Uganda, Zambia, Rwanda, and Malawi.

The torch of uhuru, or liberty, passes through a village on Independence Day.

Into the Future

Tanzania faces its fifth decade of independence with a host of major problems. But it also has a history of major social accomplishments. The education, health care, sanitation, and nutrition of the average Tanzanian have increased dramatically since the day climbers placed a torch on the peak of Mount Kilimanjaro to celebrate Tanzania's independence.

Tanzanians hoped that the light from this torch would inspire other African nations in their quest for independence. This desire to cooperate with and help other African nations has given Tanzania great importance on the African continent. Tanzania helped to topple the hated Ugandan dictator Idi Amin, and it has helped develop regional organizations like the Southern African Development Coordination Conference (SADCC).

Tanzania has played this large role on the African continent because of Julius Nyerere. He led the country to independence, helped forge its political and economic structure, and governed continuously from 1964 until 1985. He stepped down peacefully, turning power over to Ali Hassan Mwinyi, who had won the presidential election.

Unlike many other African leaders, Nyerere had a clear vision of his country's future and he worked hard to make it a reality. Nyerere wanted a society that gave equal opportunity to all people, regardless of ethnic background or sex. He wanted to end poverty and to provide Tanzanians with access to basic necessities, such as clean drinking water and health care.

To accomplish these goals, Nyerere proposed that Tanzanians adopt a socialist economy and a one-party political system. During his period as president, most of his proposals were put into practice. The government controlled industry and business. Agriculture was organized on a cooperative basis (all village members owned and worked together on the village fields). There was only one political party, the Chama Cha Mapinduzi or Revolutionary party.

However, Nyerere's programs did not achieve the results he wanted. By 1986, Tanzania was far from self-reliant. In fact, it depended heavily on foreign aid, loans, and food imports to keep its economy working and its people fed. The debt from foreign loans was over $2 billion. Most Tanzanians were still very poor by world standards. Lack of money left roads and bridges in disrepair, making transportation difficult.

In 1986, Nyerere's successor, President Mwinyi, changed many of Nyerere's policies and began a market-oriented economic policy. Government control of the economy was reduced. Tanzanians were allowed to organize political parties, and in 1995 the country held a multiparty election. The new president, Benjamin Mkapa, has continued the policies President Mwinyi originated.

Although the new policies ended a long period of economic stagnation, Tanzania remains one of the poorest countries in the world. Its foreign debt has passed the $6 billion mark, and it imports $1.4 billion of goods each year, while exporting only $462 million. Yet Tanzanians are still inspired by their young nation's independence and their hopes for the future. Many believe that the torch raised on Mount Kilimanjaro on independence day will continue to shine its rays of hope in the coming years.

‹G L O S S A R Y›

Akida | An Arab or Swahili appointed as an assistant to a German district officer during German colonial rule.

Australopithecus | Early ancestors of man whose fossil remains have been found in many parts of Tanzania. They lived from 2 million to 1 million years ago.

Masika | The heavy rains that fall between mid-March and the end of May.

Moran | Also called *ilmurran*. In the Masai system of age-grades, moran includes young adult men from age 16 to the mid-20s or 30.

Mvuli | The light rains that fall from October to December.

Ngai | The Masai god, from the word for "sky" and "air."

Swahili | The people, language, and culture that resulted from the intermarriage of Africans with Arab traders from the coastal islands.

Tsetse fly | A fly that carries diseases that are harmful to humans and fatal to livestock. Much of Tanzania is unsuitable for farming because of the tsetse fly.

Uhuru | Swahili for "independence." It was the goal and rallying cry of the Tanganyika African National Union (TANU).

Ujamaa | Swahili for "togetherness." Ujamaa are communal farming villages sponsored by the government. Under the ujamaa system, villagers work together on shared farmland.

◄INDEX►

Hindus 76
hominids 29
Homo habilis 30
Homo sapiens 30
hut tax 41

I

ilmurran 72
imperialism 35
Indian Ocean 24
industry 99–101
International Monetary Fund (IMF) 69, 101
"The Intruder" 84
Islam 76

J

judicial systems 89
Jumbe, Aboud 67, 68

K

Kagera Salient 68
Kalahari 31
Karume, Abeid 64–67
Kawawa Rashidi 63
Kenya 21, 102
Khoikhoi 31
Khoisan 31, 71
Kinjinktile 42

L

labor unions 64
Laetoli 30
Lake Natron 22
Lake Nyasa 25
Lake Tanganyika 22, 25
Lake Victoria 22, 23, 25, 31
League of Nations 43
Leakey, Louis 29

Leakey, Mary 29
Legislative Council 45, 52

M

Mafia 22
Maji Maji Rebellion 42
Makonde 83
Malagarasi River 72
Malawi 21, 25
Masai people 31, 72, 73
Masai Steppe 73
masika 27
Mazrui clan 74
Mkapa, Benjamin 69, 106
Mkwawa 37
monsoons 26
moran 72
Mount Kilimanjaro 17, 22, 80, 105, 106
Mount Meru 22, 23, 80
Mozambique 21, 34
Mugabe, Robert 68
mvuli 27
Mwanza 23
Mwinyi, Ali Hassan 18–19, 68, 69, 87, 98, 106

N

National Assembly 88
National Union of Tanganyika Workers 64
Ngai 73
Nilotes 31, 71
Nkomo, Joshua 68
Nutcracker Man 30
Nyakusa 75
Nyerere, Julius 17, 48, 49, 51, 53, 63, 64, 65, 67, 69, 95, 96–97, 101, 105, 106

O

Okello, John 64, 65
Olduvai Gorge 22, 29, 30

PICTURE CREDITS

Agency for International Development: pp. 23, 32–33, 73, 86, 90, 94; Ettagale Blauer: p. 51; AP/Wide World Photos: pp. 80–81; Dennis Degnan: pp. 50 (above and below), 52 (above), 53, 54, 55 (below), 56; International Labour Office: pp. 18, 70, 78; Jason Laure: p. 49; Carpenter Collection, Library of Congress: pp. 36, 38–39, 43, 46, 58–59; Elisofon Archives, National Museum of African Art: pp. 2, 84; David Neigus: pp. 14, 28, 79, 102, 104; New York Public Library: pp. 40–41; Peace Corps: p. 75; Antonio Rossi: pp. 51, 52–53 (below), 54–55 (above); UNESCO: p. 88; United Nations Food and Agricultural Administration: pp. 16, 20, 24–25, 96–97, 98, 100; United Republic of Tanzania: pp. 62, 67; UPI/Bettmann Newsphotos: p. 65.